SandCastle 3

Vowel Blends

ai

Mary Elizabeth Salzmann

ABDO
Publishing Company

Published by SandCastle™, an imprint of ABDO Publishing Company, 4940 Viking Drive, Edina, Minnesota 55435.

Printed in the United States.

Cover and interior photo credits: Eyewire Images, Digital Stock, Digital Vision, PhotoDisc, Stockbyte

Library of Congress Cataloging-in-Publication Data

Salzmann, Mary Elizabeth, 1968-
   Ai / Mary Elizabeth Salzmann.
     p. cm. -- (Vowel blends)
   ISBN 1-57765-453-6
    1. Readers (Primary) [1. English language--Phonetics.] I. Title.

PE1119 .S234214 2001
428.1--dc21

00-055853

The SandCastle concept, content, and reading method have been reviewed and approved by a national advisory board including literacy specialists, librarians, elementary school teachers, early childhood education professionals, and parents.

Let Us Know

After reading the book, SandCastle would like you to tell us your stories about reading. What is your favorite page? Was there something hard that you needed help with? Share the ups and downs of learning to read. We want to hear from you! To get posted on the ABDO Publishing Company Web site, send us email at:

sandcastle@abdopub.com

About SandCastle™
Nonfiction books for the beginning reader

- Basic concepts of phonics are incorporated with integrated language methods of reading instruction. Most words are short, and phrases, letter sounds, and word sounds are repeated.

- Readability is determined by the number of words in each sentence, the number of characters in each word, and word lists based on curriculum frameworks.

- Full-color photography reinforces word meanings and concepts.

- "Words I Can Read" list at the end of each book teaches basic elements of grammar, helps the reader recognize the words in the text, and builds vocabulary.

- Reading levels are indicated by the number of flags on the castle.

Look for more SandCastle books
in these three reading levels:

Level 1 (one flag)	**Level 2** (two flags)	**Level 3** (three flags)

Grades Pre-K to K 5 or fewer words per page	**Grades K to 1** 5 to 10 words per page	**Grades 1 to 2** 10 to 15 words per page

ai

Raisa has fun sending
e-mail to her best friend
Hailey.

ai

Mikhail is waiting for his turn to play in the game.

ai

Kaila likes it when her mom braids her hair in the morning.

Kailyn raises her hand in class.

She knows the right answer.

Blain pretends he is riding the rails on his toy train.

Blair plays with a pair of airplanes.

He pretends they fly to Spain.

ai

Gail and Aiden are sailing with their mom and dad in Jamaica.

17

Aimon fills his pail at the beach.

It holds many grains of sand.

19

What does **Ai**nsley wear to
rem**ai**n dry in the r**ai**n?

(r**ai**ncoat)

21

Words I Can Read

Nouns

A noun is a person, place, or thing

airplanes (AIR-planez) p. 15

answer (AN-sur) p. 11

beach (BEECH) p. 19

class (KLASS) p. 11

dad (DAD) p. 17

e-mail (EE-mayl) p. 5

friend (FREND) p. 5

fun (FUHN) p. 5

game (GAME) p. 7

grains (GRAYNZ) p. 19

hair (HAIR) p. 9

hand (HAND) p. 11

mom (MOM) pp. 9, 17

morning (MOR-ning) p. 9

pail (PAYL) p. 19

pair (PAIR) p. 15

rails (RAYLZ) p. 13

rain (RAYN) p. 21

raincoat (RAYN-koht) p. 21

sand (SAND) p. 19

train (TRANE) p. 13

turn (TURN) p. 7

Proper Nouns

A proper noun is the name
of a person, place, or thing

Aiden (AYD-en) p. 17

Aimon (AYM-on) p. 19

Ainsley (AYNZ-lee) p. 21

Blain (BLAYN) p. 13

Blair (BLARE) p. 15

Gail (GAYL) p. 17

Hailey (HAYL-ee) p. 5

Jamaica (juh-MAY-cuh) p. 17

Kaila (KAYL-uh) p. 9

Kailyn (KAY-lin) p. 11

Mikhail (mik-HAYL) p. 7

Raisa (RAYZ-uh) p. 5

Spain (SPAYN) p. 15

Pronouns

A pronoun is a word that replaces a noun

he (HEE) pp. 13, 15
it (IT) p. 9, 19

she (SHEE) p. 11
they (THAY) p. 15

what (WUHT) p. 21

Verbs

A verb is an action or being word

are (AR) p. 17
braids (BRAYDZ) p. 9
does (DUHZ) p. 21
fills (FILZ) p. 19
fly (FLYE) p. 15
has (HAZ) p. 5
holds (HOHLDZ) p. 19

is (IZ) pp. 7, 13
knows (NOHZ) p. 11
likes (LIKESS) p. 9
play (PLAY) p. 7
plays (PLAYZ) p. 15
pretends (pree-TENDZ) pp. 13, 15
raises (RAYZ-ez) p. 11

remain (ri-MAYN) p. 21
riding (RIDE-ing) p. 13
sailing (SAYL-ing) p. 17
sending (SEND-ing) p. 5
waiting (WATE-ing) p. 7
wear (WAIR) p. 21

Adjectives

An adjective describes something

best (BEST) p. 5
dry (DRYE) p. 21
her (HUR) pp. 5, 9, 11

his (HIZ) pp. 7, 13, 19
many (MEN-ee) p. 19
right (RITE) p. 11

their (THAIR) p. 17
toy (TOI) p. 13

Glossary

grains – Very small pieces or amounts of something, such as sand or salt.

pail – A plastic, wooden, or metal container with a handle.

pair – Two things that match or go together.

rails – The steel bars that guide the wheels of a train.

More ai Words

affair	explain	paid
afraid	fail	pain
aid	fair	quail
chair	gain	snail
claim	maize	stair
dairy	nail	tail

ML

10/21